Abundant Heart

Five-year
Expressions of Gratitude

Wanda Strange

Cultivate a grateful heart!

Wanda Strange

DEDICATION

My siblings
Mike, Patty, Lisa
Your love encourages me
to be a better person. .

ACKNOWLEDGMENTS

Thank you, Lisa Bell, for your continued support in all my
endeavors
and your independent publishing expertise.
Thank you to my prayer warriors, who undergird my efforts.
Thank you to Karen who planted the seed of creating
this five-year journal.

Choosing Which Wolf to Feed

An often-repeated Cherokee Indian legend vividly illustrates the struggle to maintain control of our thoughts, emotions, and actions.

The old Cherokee instructs his grandson. "A battle rages inside me, you, and every other person on earth. It is a terrible fight between two wolves. One displays anger, envy, sorrow, greed, arrogance self-pity, guilt, resentment, inferiority, lies, false pride, superiority, and ego.

The other chooses characteristics of joy, peace, love, hope, serenity, humility, kindness, benevolence, empathy, generosity truth, compassion, and faith."

The grandson inquires, "Which wolf will win?"

The grandfather simply replies, "The one you feed."

We live in a stress-filled, anxiety-producing world. The news media reports tragedies and strife daily. The crises get personal. Layoffs – divorce – health concerns accidents – caregiver stress – grief and loss – chronic pain – finances – fractured relationships – on and on.

Negative thoughts cause us to spiral into a pit, creating anxiety, anger, and an array of damaging emotions. Left unchecked, this pattern of thinking leads to depression and self-destructive behavior, side-tracking our goal of living life to the fullest.

Rachel Naomi Remen describes the problem of maintaining balance in a chaotic world. "The expectation that we can be immersed in suffering and loss daily and not be touched by it, is an unrealistic as expecting to be able to walk through water without getting wet. "

Those engaged in the helping professions are particularly vulnerable to compassion fatigue or burnout. However, every individual faces the challenge of balancing a *poor pitiful me* attitude with *abundantly joyous living.*

Employing a few basic tools, we can redirect our thoughts and win the battle. Gratitude provides one of the most powerful and effective of these tools.

We choose daily which wolf we will feed.

Scientifically Proven Benefits of Gratitude

- Gratitude improves emotional life
  - Promotes happiness
  - Reduces symptoms of depression
  - Increases resilience
  - Improves self-esteem
- Gratitude improves physical health
  - Improves sleep
  - Encourages physical exercise/activity
  - Reduces pain
  - Lowers blood pressure
  - Strengthens the immune system
  - Lowers stress
  - Activate the healing relaxation response
- Gratitude improves social interactions
  - Promotes understanding and compassion
  - Improves relationships
  - Creates positive feedback loops
- Gratitude improves professional skills
  - Improves decision making
  - Improves goal achievement
  - Promotes improved social behavior
  - Develops leadership capability
  - Promotes creativity
  - Promotes productivity
- Gratitude molds personality
  - Induces humility
  - Reduces self-focus and self-centered behavior,
  - Develops the desire to be kind and helpful
  - Increases spirituality
  - Reduces materialistic thinking
  - Encourages optimism.

((https://www.njlifehacks.com/gratitude-benefits/))

The dictionary defines gratitude as the quality of being thankful, a readiness to show appreciation for and return kindness. Most people use thankfulness and gratitude interchangeably. For me, though gratitude encompasses thankfulness, it speaks more to developing a consistent attitude of being appreciative for all the good things in life – great and small.

John Claypool wrote *Tracks of a Fellow Struggler* when his young daughter was diagnosed, treated and succumbed to leukemia. He employed gratitude as a path through days of struggle, grief and loss. He faced a choice – gratitude for the time and memories he shared with his daughter over sinking into a life of bitterness and anger.

Claypool wrote, "There is something about gratitude that has a way of multiplying our sense of resources. It is the secret of creative coping. Of all the options we have, it is perhaps the most creative and the most gracious of all."

Experts agree. They point to gratitude as an excellent coping mechanism. Research recognizes the many benefits of a grateful spirit.

So, how do we develop a grateful heart?

Christmas 2013, my friend and colleague gave me a five-year gratitude journal. I committed to the practice of journaling one gratitude thought each day. The more I viewed life through a lens of thanksgiving, the more grateful I felt. After completion of the five-year journey, it serves as a reminder of the many blessings in my life. As I read the previous years' entries, I recall special people and events of my life.

In this journal, I share reflections from my own gratitude journal as well as scripture references and quotes from many authors.

Creating this journal blessed me. Many of the quotes originate from people who found reasons to praise in the midst of unthinkable pain and suffering. By collecting these expressions of praise and gratitude from a variety of authors, my sense of thankfulness deepened.

Start whenever you choose. On each day, record one thought, person, or object for which you are grateful. You may use the scripture references or the quotes to inspire your personal reflections.

Choose to feed your positive spirit. Fill these pages with simple observations on some days and *aha moments* on others. As you develop the habit of consistently journaling the blessings you observe in your own life, I pray this tool encourages you to develop an attitude of gratitude and helps you find purpose and joy in life's journey.

Abundant Blessings,

Wanda Strange.

January 1

It is of the LORD's mercies that we are not consumed, because his compassions fail not. They are new every morning: great is thy faithfulness. *Lamentations 3: 22-23 KJV*

20..
_____
_____
_____
_____

20..
_____
_____
_____
_____

20..
_____
_____
_____
_____

20..
_____
_____
_____
_____

20..
_____
_____
_____
_____

January 2
A basic law: the more you practice the art of thankfulness,
the more you have to be thankful for.
Norman Vincent Peale

20..

_____

_____

_____

_____

20..

_____

_____

_____

_____

20..

_____

_____

_____

_____

20..

_____

_____

_____

_____

20..

_____

_____

_____

_____

January 3
Pushing aside negative thoughts,
I choose to focus on the blessings of my life.
Wanda Strange

20..
_____
_____
_____
_____

20..
_____
_____
_____
_____

20..
_____
_____
_____
_____

20..
_____
_____
_____
_____

20..
_____
_____
_____
_____

January 4

Gratitude bestows reverence, allowing us to encounter everyday
epiphanies, those transcendent moments of awe that change forever how
we experience life and the world.

John Milton

20..

_____

20..

_____

20..

_____

20..

_____

20..

_____

January 5
This a wonderful day.
I've never seen this one before.
Maya Angelou

20..

_____

_____

_____

_____

20..

_____

_____

_____

_____

20..

_____

_____

_____

_____

20..

_____

_____

_____

_____

20..

_____

_____

_____

_____

January 6

I will praise thee; for I am fearfully and wonderfully made: marvellous
are thy works; and that my soul knoweth right well.

Psalm 139:14 KJV

20..
_____
_____
_____
_____

20..
_____
_____
_____
_____

20..
_____
_____
_____
_____

20..
_____
_____
_____
_____

20..
_____
_____
_____
_____

January 7

Sunrise – Sunset – Seasons. The rhythms of nature
give structure to life. Celebrate life.
Wanda Strange

20.._____

_____

_____

_____

20.._____

_____

_____

_____

20.._____

_____

_____

_____

20.._____

_____

_____

_____

20.._____

_____

_____

_____

January 8

In ordinary life, we hardly realize that we receive a great deal more than
we give, and that it is only with gratitude that life becomes rich.
Dietrich Bonhoeffer

20..

20..

20..

20..

20..

January 9
Gratitude turns what we have
into enough.
Anonymous

20..

20..

20..

20..

20..

January 10
Piglet noticed that even though he had a Very Small Heart, it could hold
a rather large amount of Gratitude.
A.A. Milne

20..

20..

20..

20..

20..

January 11

Joy is prayer; joy is strength, joy is love. God loves a cheerful giver. The best way we can show our gratitude to God and the people is to accept everything with joy. *Mother Teresa*

20..

_____

_____

_____

20..

_____

_____

_____

20..

_____

_____

_____

20..

_____

_____

_____

20..

_____

_____

_____

January 12

There is something about gratitude that has a way of multiplying our sense of resources. It is the secret of creative coping. Of all the options we have, it is perhaps the most creative and the most gracious of all.

John Claypool

20..
_____
_____
_____
_____

20..
_____
_____
_____
_____

20..
_____
_____
_____
_____

20..
_____
_____
_____
_____

20..
_____
_____
_____
_____

January 13
The more I view life through a lens of gratitude,
the more grateful I feel.
Wanda Strange

20.. _____
_____
_____
_____

20.. _____
_____
_____
_____

20.. _____
_____
_____
_____

20.. _____
_____
_____
_____

20.. _____
_____
_____
_____

January 14
Feeling gratitude and not expressing is like
wrapping a present and not giving it.
William Arthur Ward

20..

_____

_____

_____

_____

20..

_____

_____

_____

_____

20..

_____

_____

_____

_____

20..

_____

_____

_____

_____

20..

_____

_____

_____

_____

January 15

When peace like a river, attendeth my way. When sorrows like sea
billows roll; Whatever my lot, Thou hast taught me to know.
It is well, it is well, with my soul.
Horatio Spafford

20..

_____

_____

_____

_____

20..

_____

_____

_____

_____

20..

_____

_____

_____

_____

20..

_____

_____

_____

_____

20..

_____

_____

_____

_____

January 16
O satisfy us early with thy mercy;
that we may rejoice and be glad all our days.
Psalm 90:14 KJV

20..

_____

_____

_____

_____

20..

_____

_____

_____

_____

20..

_____

_____

_____

_____

20..

_____

_____

_____

_____

20..

_____

_____

_____

_____

January 17
I am thankful for the grace to trust
even when the answer is not what I desired or expected.
Wanda Strange

20..

20..

20..

20..

20..

January 18
We often take for granted the very things
that most deserve our gratitude.
Cynthia Ozick

20..
_____
_____
_____
_____

20..
_____
_____
_____
_____

20..
_____
_____
_____
_____

20..
_____
_____
_____
_____

20..
_____
_____
_____
_____

January 19

I've had a remarkable life. I seem to be in such good places at the right time. You know, if you were to ask me to sum my life up in one word –
gratitude.
Dietrich Bonhoeffer

20..

20..

20..

20..

20..

January 20

Today I choose to live with gratitude for the love that fills my heart,
the peace that rests within my spirit,
and the voice of hope that says all things are possible.

Anonymous

20..

20..

20..

20..

20..

January 21

If a fellow isn't thankful for what he's got,
he isn't likely to be thankful for what he's going to get.
Frank A. Clark

20..

20..

20..

20..

20..

January 22

Be careful for nothing; but in every thing by prayer and supplication
with thanksgiving let your requests be made known unto God.
Philippians 4:6 KJV

20..
_____
_____
_____
_____

20..
_____
_____
_____
_____

20..
_____
_____
_____
_____

20..
_____
_____
_____
_____

20..
_____
_____
_____
_____

January 23

Life is a gift! Every sunrise affords the opportunity to celebrate life.
Our next breath is not promised. Don't take it for granted.
Wanda Strange

20.._____

_____

_____

_____

20.._____

_____

_____

_____

20.._____

_____

_____

_____

20.._____

_____

_____

_____

20.._____

_____

_____

_____

January 24

Yesterday is history, tomorrow is a mystery,
and today is a gift; that's why they call it the present.
Eleanor Roosevelt

20..
_____
_____
_____
_____

20..
_____
_____
_____
_____

20..
_____
_____
_____
_____

20..
_____
_____
_____
_____

20..
_____
_____
_____
_____

January 25
Gratitude is a currency that we can mint for ourselves,
and spend without fear of bankruptcy.
Fred De Witt Van Amburgh

20.._____
_____
_____
_____

20.._____
_____
_____
_____

20.._____
_____
_____
_____

20.._____
_____
_____
_____

20.._____
_____
_____
_____

January 26

I thank God for his blessings, and the mercies He's bestowed.
I'm drinking from my saucer, 'Cause my cup has overflowed.
John Paul Moore

20..
_____
_____
_____
_____

20..
_____
_____
_____
_____

20..
_____
_____
_____
_____

20..
_____
_____
_____
_____

20..
_____
_____
_____
_____

January 27

Each day provides the opportunity to fulfill God's purpose for my life. He has a plan for each phase of life. As long as I live and breathe, there is something for me to do. *Wanda Strange*

20.. _____
_____
_____
_____

20.. _____
_____
_____
_____

20.. _____
_____
_____
_____

20.. _____
_____
_____
_____

20.. _____
_____
_____
_____

January 28

For I know the thoughts that I think toward you, saith the LORD,
thoughts of peace, and not of evil, to give you an expected end.
Jeremiah 29:11 KJV

20..

_____

_____

_____

_____

20..

_____

_____

_____

_____

20..

_____

_____

_____

_____

20..

_____

_____

_____

_____

20..

_____

_____

_____

_____

January 29
God whispers in our pleasures,
speaks to us in our conscience, but shouts in our pains.
It is His megaphone to rouse a deaf world.
C. S. Lewis

20..

20..

20..

20..

20..

January 30
This morning I witnessed an amazing sunrise – morning broke – a brief
moment in time – very grateful I didn't miss it.
Wanda Strange

20..
_____
_____
_____
_____

20..
_____
_____
_____
_____

20..
_____
_____
_____
_____

20..
_____
_____
_____
_____

20..
_____
_____
_____
_____

January 31
Retire from the world each day to some private spot… Stay in the secret
place till the surrounding noises begin to fade out of your heart and a
sense of God's presence envelopes you.
A. W. Tozer

20.. _____
_____
_____
_____

20.. _____
_____
_____
_____

20.. _____
_____
_____
_____

20.. _____
_____
_____
_____

20.. _____
_____
_____
_____

February 1

Be still, and know that I am God: I will be exalted among the heathen, I will be exalted in the earth.

Psalm 46:10 KJV

20..

_____

_____

_____

_____

20..

_____

_____

_____

_____

20..

_____

_____

_____

_____

20..

_____

_____

_____

_____

20..

_____

_____

_____

_____

February 2
Worry does not empty tomorrow of its sorrow.
It empties today of its strength.
Corrie Ten Boom

20..

20..

20..

20..

20..

February 3
In every thing give thanks:
for this is the will of God in Christ Jesus concerning you.
1 Thessalonians 5:18 KJV

20..

20..

20..

20..

20..

February 4

Do not spoil what you have by desiring what you have not; remember that what you now have was once among the things you only hoped for.

Epicurus

20..

20..

20..

20..

20..

February 5
We can complain because rose bushes have thorns,
or rejoice because thorns have roses.
Alphonse Karr, <u>A Tour Round My Garden</u>

20..

_____

20..

_____

20..

_____

20..

_____

20..

_____

February 6

Cultivate the habit of being grateful for every good thing that comes to you, and to give thanks continuously. And because all things have contributed to your advancement, you should include all things in your gratitude. *Ralph Waldo Emerson*

20..

20..

20..

20..

20..

February 7

Let gratitude be the pillow upon which you kneel to say your nightly prayer. And let faith be the bridge you build to overcome evil and welcome good. *Maya Angelou*

20..
_____
_____
_____
_____

20..
_____
_____
_____
_____

20..
_____
_____
_____
_____

20..
_____
_____
_____
_____

20..
_____
_____
_____
_____

February 8
We must find time to stop and
thank the people who make a difference in our lives.
John F. Kennedy

20.. _____
_____
_____
_____

20.. _____
_____
_____
_____

20.. _____
_____
_____
_____

20.. _____
_____
_____
_____

20.. _____
_____
_____
_____

February 9

The unthankful heart discovers no mercies; but the thankful heart will find, in every hour, some heavenly blessings.

Henry Ward Beecher

20..

_____

_____

_____

_____

20..

_____

_____

_____

_____

20..

_____

_____

_____

_____

20..

_____

_____

_____

_____

20..

_____

_____

_____

_____

February 10
O give thanks unto the LORD; for he is good;
for his mercy endureth for ever.
1 Chronicles 16:34 KJV

20..

20..

20..

20..

20..

February 11

If you look at the world, you'll be distressed.
If you look within, you'll be depressed.
But if you look at Christ, you'll be at rest.
Corrie Ten Boom

20..

20..

20..

20..

20..

February 12
For each new morning with its light, For rest and shelter of the night,
For health and food, for love and friends,
For everything Thy goodness sends.
Ralph Emerson

20..
_____
_____
_____
_____

20..
_____
_____
_____
_____

20..
_____
_____
_____
_____

20..
_____
_____
_____
_____

20..
_____
_____
_____
_____

February 13
God gave you a gift of 84,600 seconds today.
Have you used one of them to say thank you?
William Arthur Ward

20..
_____
_____
_____
_____

20..
_____
_____
_____
_____

20..
_____
_____
_____
_____

20..
_____
_____
_____
_____

20..
_____
_____
_____
_____

February 14

Jesus said unto him, Thou shalt love the Lord thy God with all thy heart,
and with all thy soul, and with all thy mind.
Matthew 22:37 KJV

20..
_____
_____
_____
_____

20..
_____
_____
_____
_____

20..
_____
_____
_____
_____

20..
_____
_____
_____
_____

20..
_____
_____
_____
_____

February 15
He who does not reflect his life back to God
in gratitude does not know himself.
Albert Schweitzer

20..
_____
_____
_____
_____

20..
_____
_____
_____
_____

20..
_____
_____
_____
_____

20..
_____
_____
_____
_____

20..
_____
_____
_____
_____

February 16

It has been said that life has treated me harshly; and sometimes I have complained in my heart because many pleasures of human experience have been withheld from me…if much has been denied me, much, very much, has been given me. *Helen Keller, The Open Door*

20..

20..

20..

20..

20..

February 17
They do not love,
that do not show their love.
William Shakespeare

20..

20..

20..

20..

20..

February 18
Grief's darkness fades in the
sunlight of thanksgiving.
Billy Graham

20..

20..

20..

20..

20..

February 19
Gratitude exclaims, very properly,
"How good of God to give me this!"
C. S. Lewis

20.. _____
_____
_____
_____

20.. _____
_____
_____
_____

20.. _____
_____
_____
_____

20.. _____
_____
_____
_____

20.. _____
_____
_____
_____

February 20
Darkness cannot drive out darkness. Only light can do that.
Hate cannot drive out hate. Only love can do that.
Martin Luther King, Jr.

20..

20..

20..

20..

20..

February 21

True friendships enrich lives. What a blessing to have friends who share history – those for whom no words are necessary – those who instinctively understand. *Wanda Strange*

20..
_____
_____
_____
_____

20..
_____
_____
_____
_____

20..
_____
_____
_____
_____

20..
_____
_____
_____
_____

20..
_____
_____
_____
_____

February 22
I thank my God upon every remembrance of you.
Always in every prayer of mine for you all making request with joy.
Philippians 1:3-4 KJV

20..

20..

20..

20..

20..

February 23
Gratitude. More aware of what you have than what you don't.
Recognizing the treasure in the simple - a child's hug, fertile soil, a
golden sunset. Relishing in the comfort of the common. *Max Lucado*

20..

20..

20..

20..

20..

February 24
A brother shares childhood memories
and grown-up dreams.
Anonymous

20..
_____
_____
_____
_____

20..
_____
_____
_____
_____

20..
_____
_____
_____
_____

20..
_____
_____
_____
_____

20..
_____
_____
_____
_____

February 25
A friend loveth at all times,
and a brother is born for adversity.
Proverbs 17:17 KJV

20..

20..

20..

20..

20..

February 26
Thank you is the best prayer that anyone could say. I say that one a lot.
Thank you expresses extreme gratitude, humility understanding.
Alice Walker

20..

20..

20..

20..

20..

February 27
Kindness is the language
which the deaf can hear and the blind can see.
Mark Twain

20..

20..

20..

20..

20..

February 28

God does not waste our time… Every experience and person can lead us to God,
and God is waiting to be found in each moment of our day, waiting for us to
allow the things and people around us to cause us to remember him.
Mia Pohlman

20..

20..

20..

20..

20..

February 29
*Happy Leap Day. A day where 'this time last year'
and 'this time next year' does not apply."*
Anonymous

20..

20..

20..

20..

20..

March 1

What hinders me from hearing is that I am taking up with other things. It is not that I will not hear God, but I am not devoted in the right place.
Oswald Chambers

20.._____
_____
_____
_____

20.._____
_____
_____
_____

20.._____
_____
_____
_____

20.._____
_____
_____
_____

20.._____
_____
_____
_____

March 2

Gratitude honors God. Gratitude is the echo of grace
as it reverberates through the hollows of the human heart.
John Piper

20..
_____
_____
_____
_____

20..
_____
_____
_____
_____

20..
_____
_____
_____
_____

20..
_____
_____
_____
_____

20..
_____
_____
_____
_____

March 3
It was one of those March days when the sun shines hot and the wind
blows cold: when it is summer in the light, and winter in the shade.
Charles Dickens

20..

_____

_____

_____

_____

20..

_____

_____

_____

_____

20..

_____

_____

_____

_____

20..

_____

_____

_____

_____

20..

_____

_____

_____

_____

March 4

For ye shall go out with joy, and be led forth with peace:
the mountains and the hills shall break forth before you into singing,
and all the trees of the field shall clap their hands.
Isaiah 55:12 KJV

20..
_____
_____
_____
_____

20..
_____
_____
_____
_____

20..
_____
_____
_____
_____

20..
_____
_____
_____
_____

20..
_____
_____
_____
_____

March 5

Great faith isn't the ability to believe long and far into the misty future.
It's simply taking God at His word and taking the next step.
Joni Eareckson Tada

20.._____

_____

_____

_____

20.._____

_____

_____

_____

20.._____

_____

_____

_____

20.._____

_____

_____

_____

20.._____

_____

_____

_____

March 6

Today is my favorite day. Yesterday, when it was tomorrow,
it was too much day for me.
Winnie the Pooh – A. A. Milne

20..

20..

20..

20..

20..

March 7
Our life is a gift from God.
What we do with that life is our gift to God.
Samuel S Sumner

20..
_____
_____
_____
_____

20..
_____
_____
_____
_____

20..
_____
_____
_____
_____

20..
_____
_____
_____
_____

20..
_____
_____
_____
_____

March 8
Family shapes us into the people we are.
We choose to incorporate the strengths of our parents and grandparents.
If wise, we learn from the mistakes of the past.
Wanda Strange

20..
_____
_____
_____
_____

20..
_____
_____
_____
_____

20..
_____
_____
_____
_____

20..
_____
_____
_____
_____

20..
_____
_____
_____
_____

March 9
There is no pit so deep,
that God's love is not deeper still.
Corrie Ten Boom

20..

20..

20..

20..

20..

March 10
The lines are fallen unto me in pleasant places;
yea, I have a goodly heritage.
Psalm 16:6 KJV

20..
_____
_____
_____
_____

20..
_____
_____
_____
_____

20..
_____
_____
_____
_____

20..
_____
_____
_____
_____

20..
_____
_____
_____
_____

March 11
March, when the days are getting long,
Let thy growing hours be strong, To set right some wintry wrong.
Caroline May 1887

20.. _____
_____
_____
_____

20.. _____
_____
_____
_____

20.. _____
_____
_____
_____

20.. _____
_____
_____
_____

20.. _____
_____
_____
_____

March 12

It isn't what you have in your pocket that makes you thankful, but what you have in your heart.

Author Unknown

20..

_____

20..

_____

20..

_____

20..

_____

20..

_____

March 13
Peach blossoms emerged this week despite an unseasonably late
Texas freeze. The beautiful blooming tree, delightful to the eyes,
promises a sweet harvest of summer fruit. *Wanda Strange*

20..

20..

20..

20..

20..

March 14

One of the first things I usually ask God when circumstances change is: "God, is there something you want to teach me through this?"
Rebecca Barlow Jordan

20..
_____
_____
_____
_____

20..
_____
_____
_____
_____

20..
_____
_____
_____
_____

20..
_____
_____
_____
_____

20..
_____
_____
_____
_____

March 15

God loves me just as I am today. He knows all my junk. He knows all my
inadequacies and lack of faith, and He loves me anyway.
However, He loves me too much to leave me the way I am.
Michelle Akers

20.. _____
_____
_____
_____

20.. _____
_____
_____
_____

20.. _____
_____
_____
_____

20.. _____
_____
_____
_____

20.. _____
_____
_____
_____

March 16
The heavens declare the glory of God;
and the firmament sheweth his handywork.
Psalm 19:1 KJV

20..

20..

20..

20..

20..

March 17

May the road rise up to meet you. May the wind be always at your
back. May the sun shine warm upon your face; the rains fall soft upon
your fields and until we meet again, may God hold you in the palm of
His hand. *Traditional Gaelic Blessing*

20..
_____
_____
_____
_____

20..
_____
_____
_____
_____

20..
_____
_____
_____
_____

20..
_____
_____
_____
_____

20..
_____
_____
_____
_____

March 18

Be Thou my Vision, O Lord of my heart; Naught be all else to me, save
that Thou art… Heart of my own heart, whatever befall,
Still be my Vision, O Ruler of all.
Traditional Christian Hymn of Irish Origin Eleanor Hull (1912)

20..
_____
_____
_____
_____

20..
_____
_____
_____
_____

20..
_____
_____
_____
_____

20..
_____
_____
_____
_____

20..
_____
_____
_____
_____

March 19

We should be astonished at the goodness of God, stunned that He
should bother to call us by name, our mouths wide open at His love,
bewildered that at his very moment we are standing on holy ground.
Brennan Manning

20.. _____

_____

_____

_____

20.. _____

_____

_____

_____

20.. _____

_____

_____

_____

20.. _____

_____

_____

_____

20.. _____

_____

_____

_____

March 20
There is a God-shaped vacuum
in every heart
Blaise Pascal

20..
_____
_____
_____
_____

20..
_____
_____
_____
_____

20..
_____
_____
_____
_____

20..
_____
_____
_____
_____

20..
_____
_____
_____
_____

March 21

Enter into his gates with thanksgiving, and into his courts with praise: be
thankful unto him, and bless his name.
Psalm 100:4 KJV

20.._____
_____
_____
_____

20.._____
_____
_____
_____

20.._____
_____
_____
_____

20.._____
_____
_____
_____

20.._____
_____
_____
_____

March 22

Grant me, O Lord, my God, a mind to know You, a heart to seek You,
wisdom to find You, conduct pleasing to You, faithful perseverance in
waiting for You, and a hope of finally embracing You. Amen.
Thomas Aquinas

20..

20..

20..

20..

20..

March 23
I have decided to stick with love.
Hate is too great a burden to bear.
Martin Luther King Jr.

20.._____
_____
_____
_____

20.._____
_____
_____
_____

20.._____
_____
_____
_____

20.._____
_____
_____
_____

20.._____
_____
_____
_____

March 24
Happiness isn't something that depends on our surroundings...
it's something we make inside ourselves.
Corrie Ten Boom

20..

20..

20..

20..

20..

March 25

In Jesus the weak are strong and the defenseless safe; they could not be more strong if they were giants, or more safe if they were in heaven. Faith gives to men on earth the protection of the God of heaven.
Charles Spurgeon

20..
_____
_____
_____
_____

20..
_____
_____
_____
_____

20..
_____
_____
_____
_____

20..
_____
_____
_____
_____

20..
_____
_____
_____
_____

March 26

Come unto me, all ye that labour and are heavy laden,
and I will give you rest. Take my yoke upon you, and learn of me;
for I am meek and lowly in heart: and ye shall find rest unto your souls.
For my yoke is easy, and my burden is light. *Matthew 11:28-30 KJV*

20..

_____

_____

_____

_____

20..

_____

_____

_____

_____

20..

_____

_____

_____

_____

20..

_____

_____

_____

_____

20..

_____

_____

_____

_____

March 27

Come and sit and ask Him whatever is on your heart.
No question is too simple. He has all the time in the world.
Come and seek the will of God. *Max Lucado*

20..

20..

20..

20..

20..

March 28

He who cannot rest, cannot work. He who cannot let go, cannot hold on.
He who cannot find footing, cannot move forward.
Harry Emerson Fosdick

20..

20..

20..

20..

20..

March 29
Prayer is the exercise of drawing
on the grace of God
Oswald Chambers

20..
_____
_____
_____
_____

20..
_____
_____
_____
_____

20..
_____
_____
_____
_____

20..
_____
_____
_____
_____

20..
_____
_____
_____
_____

March 30
No matter your relationship with your mother,
you will miss her when she is gone.
Wanda Strange

20..

20..

20..

20..

20..

March 31

But they that wait upon the LORD shall renew their strength; they shall mount up with wings as eagles; they shall run, and not be weary; and they shall walk, and not faint. *Isaiah 40:31 KJV*

20..
_____

_____

_____

_____

20..
_____

_____

_____

_____

20..
_____

_____

_____

_____

20..
_____

_____

_____

_____

20..
_____

_____

_____

_____

April 1
Where flowers bloom
so does hope.
Lady Bird Johnson

20..

20..

20..

20..

20..

April 2
The earth laughs
in flowers.
Ralph Waldo Emerson

20..
_____
_____
_____
_____

20..
_____
_____
_____
_____

20..
_____
_____
_____
_____

20..
_____
_____
_____
_____

20..
_____
_____
_____
_____

April 3

If we had no winter,
the spring would not be so pleasant.
Anne Bradstreet

20..

20..

20..

20..

20..

April 4
Spring is the time
of plans and projects
Leo Tolstoy

20.._____
_____
_____
_____

20.._____
_____
_____
_____

20.._____
_____
_____
_____

20.._____
_____
_____
_____

20.._____
_____
_____
_____

April 5

Consider the lilies how they grow: they toil not, they spin not; and yet I say unto you, that Solomon in all his glory was not arrayed like one of these. *Luke 12:27 KJV*

20..
_____
_____
_____
_____

20..
_____
_____
_____
_____

20..
_____
_____
_____
_____

20..
_____
_____
_____
_____

20..
_____
_____
_____
_____

April 6

When you rise in the morning, give thanks for the light, for your life, for your strength. Give thanks for your food and for the joy of living. If you see no reason to give thanks, the fault lies in yourself. *Tecumseh*

20..

20..

20..

20..

20..

April 7
Joy in looking and comprehending
is nature's most beautiful gift.
Albert Einstein

20..
_____
_____
_____
_____

20..
_____
_____
_____
_____

20..
_____
_____
_____
_____

20..
_____
_____
_____
_____

20..
_____
_____
_____
_____

April 8

I cannot even imagine where I would be today were it not for that
handful of friends who have given me a heart full of joy.
Let's face it, friends make life a lot more fun.
Charles R. Swindoll

20..

20..

20..

20..

20..

April 9
Nobody understands another's sorrow,
and nobody another's joy.
Franz Schubert

20..
_____
_____
_____
_____

20..
_____
_____
_____
_____

20..
_____
_____
_____
_____

20..
_____
_____
_____
_____

20..
_____
_____
_____
_____

April 10
Gratitude can transform common days into thanksgivings,
turn routine jobs into joy,
and change ordinary opportunities into blessings.
William Arthur Ward

20..

20..

20..

20..

20..

April 11

The best news of the Christian gospel is that the supremely glorious Creator of the universe has acted in Jesus Christ's death and resurrection to remove every obstacle between us and himself so that we may find everlasting joy in seeing and savoring his infinite beauty. *John Piper*

20..

20..

20..

20..

20..

April 12
Look deep into nature,
and then you will understand everything better.
Albert Einstein

20..
_____

20..
_____

20..
_____

20..
_____

20..
_____

April 13
Adopt the pace of nature:
her secret is patience.
Ralph Waldo Emerson

20..
_____
_____
_____
_____

20..
_____
_____
_____
_____

20..
_____
_____
_____
_____

20..
_____
_____
_____
_____

20..
_____
_____
_____
_____

April 14

We need to find God, and he cannot be found in noise and restlessness.
God is the friend of silence. See how nature - trees, flowers, grass- grows
in silence; see the stars, the moon and the sun, how they move in
silence... We need silence to be able to touch souls. *Mother Teresa*

20..

20..

20..

20..

20..

April 15
Thou art my hiding place and my shield:
I hope in thy word.
Psalm 119:114 KJV

20..

20..

20..

20..

20..

April 16
Gratitude is the fairest blossom
which springs from the soul.
Henry Ward Beecher

20..

20..

20..

20..

20..

April 17
Never lose the childlike wonder. Show gratitude...
Don't complain; just work harder... Never give up.
Randy Pausch

20..
_____
_____
_____
_____

20..
_____
_____
_____
_____

20..
_____
_____
_____
_____

20..
_____
_____
_____
_____

20..
_____
_____
_____
_____

April 18

At times, our own light goes out and is rekindled by a spark from another person. Each of us has cause to think with deep gratitude of those who have lighted the flame within us.

Albert Schweitzer

20..

_____

_____

_____

_____

20..

_____

_____

_____

_____

20..

_____

_____

_____

_____

20..

_____

_____

_____

_____

20..

_____

_____

_____

_____

April 19
Gratitude is the healthiest of all human emotions.
The more you express gratitude for what you have,
the more likely you will have even more to express gratitude for.
Zig Ziglar

20..

20..

20..

20..

20..

April 20
Praise ye the LORD. Praise God in his sanctuary:
praise him in the firmament of his power…
Let everything that hath breath praise the LORD. Praise ye the LORD.
Psalm 150: 1, 6 KJV

20.. _____
_____
_____
_____

20.. _____
_____
_____
_____

20.. _____
_____
_____
_____

20.. _____
_____
_____
_____

20.. _____
_____
_____
_____

April 21
I live by two words:
tenacity and gratitude.
Henry Winkler

20..

20..

20..

20..

20..

April 22
Feeling gratitude isn't born in us – it's something we are taught,
and in turn, we teach our children.
Joyce Brothers

20.._____
_____
_____
_____

20.._____
_____
_____
_____

20.._____
_____
_____
_____

20.._____
_____
_____
_____

20.._____
_____
_____
_____

April 23
It is not joy that makes us grateful,
it is gratitude that makes us joyful.
David Steindl-Rast

20..

20..

20..

20..

20..

April 24
Gratitude doesn't change the scenery. It merely washes clean the glass
you look through so you can clearly see the colors.
Richelle E. Goodric, poet

20..

20..

20..

20..

20..

April 25
It is only with gratitude that life becomes rich.
Dietrich Bonhoeffer,
German pastor and theologian

20..
_____
_____
_____
_____

20..
_____
_____
_____
_____

20..
_____
_____
_____
_____

20..
_____
_____
_____
_____

20..
_____
_____
_____
_____

April 26
There are always flowers
for those who want to see them.
Henri Matisse, French artist

20..

20..

20..

20..

20..

April 27
There are only two ways to live your life.
One is as though nothing is a miracle.
The other is as though everything is a miracle.
Albert Einstein

20..

20..

20..

20..

20..

April 28
When we give cheerfully and accept gratefully,
everyone is blessed.
Maya Angelou

20..
_____
_____
_____
_____

20..
_____
_____
_____
_____

20..
_____
_____
_____
_____

20..
_____
_____
_____
_____

20..
_____
_____
_____
_____

April 29
As long as this exists, this sunshine and this cloudless sky,
and as long as I can enjoy it, how can I be sad?
Anne Frank

20..
_____
_____
_____
_____

20..
_____
_____
_____
_____

20..
_____
_____
_____
_____

20..
_____
_____
_____
_____

20..
_____
_____
_____
_____

April 30
An early-morning walk is a
blessing for the whole day.
Henry David Thoreau

20..
_____
_____
_____
_____

20..
_____
_____
_____
_____

20..
_____
_____
_____
_____

20..
_____
_____
_____
_____

20..
_____
_____
_____
_____

May 1
The music is not in the notes,
but in the silence in between.
Wolfgang Amadeus Mozart

20..

20..

20..

20..

20..

May 2
Gratitude changes the pangs of memory
into a tranquil joy.
Dietrich Bonhoeffer

20..
_____
_____
_____
_____

20..
_____
_____
_____
_____

20..
_____
_____
_____
_____

20..
_____
_____
_____
_____

20..
_____
_____
_____
_____

May 3
Among the things you can give and still keep are your word,
a smile, and a grateful heart.
Zig Ziglar

20..

20..

20..

20..

20..

May 4
Life has no blessing
like a prudent friend.
Euripides

20..
_____
_____
_____
_____

20..
_____
_____
_____
_____

20..
_____
_____
_____
_____

20..
_____
_____
_____
_____

20..
_____
_____
_____
_____

May 5

I awoke this morning with devout thanksgiving
for my friends, the old and the new.
Ralph Waldo Emerson

20..

20..

20..

20..

20..

May 6
Sometimes the best way to appreciate something
is to be without it for a while.
Unknown

20..

20..

20..

20..

20..

May 7
Think with great gratitude of those
who have lighted the flame within us.
Albert Schweitzer

20..

20..

20..

20..

20..

May 8
Happy is the man who finds a true friend,
and far happier is he who finds that true friend in his wife.
Franz Schubert

20.._____
_____
_____
_____

20.._____
_____
_____
_____

20.._____
_____
_____
_____

20.._____
_____
_____
_____

20.._____
_____
_____
_____

May 9
If you have built castles in the air, your work need not be lost, that is
where they should be. Now put the foundations under them.
Henry David Thoreau

20..
_____
_____
_____
_____

20..
_____
_____
_____
_____

20..
_____
_____
_____
_____

20..
_____
_____
_____
_____

20..
_____
_____
_____
_____

May 10

If you're more fortunate than others,
build a longer table, not a taller fence.
Unknown

20..

_____

_____

_____

20..

_____

_____

_____

20..

_____

_____

_____

20..

_____

_____

_____

20..

_____

_____

_____

May 11

The best way to show my gratitude to God
is to accept everything, even my problems, with joy.
Mother Teresa

20..
_____
_____
_____
_____

20..
_____
_____
_____
_____

20..
_____
_____
_____
_____

20..
_____
_____
_____
_____

20..
_____
_____
_____
_____

May 12
O Lord that lends me life,
Lend me a heart replete with thankfulness!
William Shakespeare

20..

20..

20..

20..

20..

May 13
Change, like sunshine, can be a friend or a foe,
a blessing or a curse, a dawn or a dusk.
William Arthur Ward

20..

20..

20..

20..

20..

May 14

Let us remember that, as much has been given us, much will be
expected from us, and that true homage comes from the heart
as well as from the lips, and shows itself in deeds.
Theodore Roosevelt

20..

20..

20..

20..

20..

May 15
Love your mistakes as much as your accomplishments.
Because without mistakes, there wouldn't be any accomplishments.
Unknown

20..

20..

20..

20..

20..

May 16
A wise man should consider that health is the greatest of
human blessings, and learn how by his own thought
to derive benefit from his illnesses.
Hippocrates

20..

20..

20..

20..

20..

May 17

I know what I'm doing. I have it all planned out — plans to take care of you, not abandon you, plans to give you the future you hope for. When you call on me, when you come and pray to me, I'll listen. When you come looking for me, you'll find me. *Jeremiah 29:11-13 The Message*

20..

20..

20..

20..

20..

May 18
The main thing that God asks for
is our attention.
Jim Cymbala

20..
_____
_____
_____
_____

20..
_____
_____
_____
_____

20..
_____
_____
_____
_____

20..
_____
_____
_____
_____

20..
_____
_____
_____
_____

May 19
A quiet place is a good place to
find God's angle on any problem.
Janette Oke

20..

20..

20..

20..

20..

145

May 20

Not being changed by prayer is sort of like standing in the middle of a spring rain without getting wet. It's hard to stand in the center of God's acceptance and love without getting it all over you. *Steve Brown*

20..
_____
_____
_____
_____

20..
_____
_____
_____
_____

20..
_____
_____
_____
_____

20..
_____
_____
_____
_____

20..
_____
_____
_____
_____

May 21
Take a moment to consider the awesome reality that the God
who spoke and created the universe is now speaking to you.
Henry T Blackaby

20..

20..

20..

20..

20..

May 22

He is the source. Of everything. Strength for your day.
Comfort for your soul. Grace for your battle. Provision for each need.
Understanding for each failure. Assistance for every encounter.
Jack Hayford

20.. _____

_____

_____

_____

20.. _____

_____

_____

_____

20.. _____

_____

_____

_____

20.. _____

_____

_____

_____

20.. _____

_____

_____

_____

May 23
God is more anxious to bless us than we are to be blessed.
More anxious to give us wisdom, strength, and peace
than we are to take them.
Richard C Halverson

20..
_____
_____
_____
_____

20..
_____
_____
_____
_____

20..
_____
_____
_____
_____

20..
_____
_____
_____
_____

20..
_____
_____
_____
_____

May 24
We aren't just thrown on this earth like dice tossed across a table.
We are lovingly placed here for a purpose.
Charles Swindoll

20..

20..

20..

20..

20..

May 25

But as it is written, Eye hath not seen, nor ear heard, neither have entered into the heart of man, the things which God hath prepared for them that love him. *1 Corinthians 2:9 KJV*

20..

_____

_____

_____

_____

20..

_____

_____

_____

_____

20..

_____

_____

_____

_____

20..

_____

_____

_____

_____

20..

_____

_____

_____

_____

May 26

Are you weak? Weary? Confused? Troubled? Pressured? How is your
relationship with God? Is it held in its place of priority? I believe the
greater the pressure, the greater your need for time alone with Him.
Kay Arthur

20.. _____
_____
_____
_____

20.. _____
_____
_____
_____

20.. _____
_____
_____
_____

20.. _____
_____
_____
_____

20.. _____
_____
_____
_____

May 27
Make within our hearts a quiet place.
We release to You our demand to see what the future holds.
We rest in You content to know only You and care in this present hour.
Peter Marshall

20..

20..

20..

20..

20..

May 28
You have made us for Yourself, O Lord,
and our heart is restless until it rests in You.
Augustine

20.. _____
_____
_____
_____

20.. _____
_____
_____
_____

20.. _____
_____
_____
_____

20.. _____
_____
_____
_____

20.. _____
_____
_____
_____

May 29
True prayer is simply a quiet, sincere, genuine conversation with God.
It is a two-way dialogue between friends.
W. Phillip Keller

20..

20..

20..

20..

20..

May 30
God sometimes seems to speak to us most intimately
when He catches us, as it were, off our guard.
C. S. Lewis

20..

20..

20..

20..

20..

May 31
Trust in the LORD with all thine heart;
and lean not unto thine own understanding.
In all thy ways acknowledge him, and he shall direct thy paths.
Proverbs 3:5-6 KJV

20..
_____
_____
_____
_____

20..
_____
_____
_____
_____

20..
_____
_____
_____
_____

20..
_____
_____
_____
_____

20..
_____
_____
_____
_____

June 1

Never take for granted any of your five senses. Sight, sound, smell,
savoring tastes, and sensation allow the us to experience life more fully.
Wanda Strange

20.. _____
_____
_____
_____

20.. _____
_____
_____
_____

20.. _____
_____
_____
_____

20.. _____
_____
_____
_____

20.. _____
_____
_____
_____

June 2
God is never in a hurry,
but He is always on time.
Rick Warren

20..
_____
_____
_____
_____

20..
_____
_____
_____
_____

20..
_____
_____
_____
_____

20..
_____
_____
_____
_____

20..
_____
_____
_____
_____

June 3
Never be afraid to trust an
unknown future to a known God.
Corrie Ten Boom

20..

20..

20..

20..

20..

June 4
Even though you may not understand how God works,
you know He does.
Max Lucado

20..

20..

20..

20..

20..

June 5
I would rather walk with God in the dark
than go alone in the light.
Mary Gardiner Brainard

20.. _____
_____
_____
_____

20.. _____
_____
_____
_____

20.. _____
_____
_____
_____

20.. _____
_____
_____
_____

20.. _____
_____
_____
_____

June 6

As I seek God's guidance for wise decisions, I gratefully acknowledge
my trust in His plan for my life – today, tomorrow and for eternity.
Wanda Strange

20..
_____
_____
_____
_____

20..
_____
_____
_____
_____

20..
_____
_____
_____
_____

20..
_____
_____
_____
_____

20..
_____
_____
_____
_____

June 7
For a day in thy courts is better than a thousand.
I had rather be a doorkeeper in the house of my God,
than to dwell in the tents of wickedness.
Psalm 84:10 KVJ

20..

20..

20..

20..

20..

June 8

All creatures of our God and King, Lift up your voice and with us sing,
Alleluia! Alleluia! Thou burning sun with golden beam,
Thou silver moon with softer gleam! O praise Him! O praise Him!
Alleluia! Alleluia! Alleluia! *Francis of Assisi*

20..

20..

20..

20..

20..

June 9

Incredible as it may seem, God wants... to be a father to us, to shield us, to protect us, to counsel us, and to guide us in our way through life.
Billy Graham

20.. _____
_____
_____
_____

20.. _____
_____
_____
_____

20.. _____
_____
_____
_____

20.. _____
_____
_____
_____

20.. _____
_____
_____
_____

June 10

There are four ways God answers prayer: No, not yet;
No, I love you too much; Yes, I thought you'd never ask;
Yes, and here's more.
Anne Lewis

20..
_____
_____
_____
_____

20..
_____
_____
_____
_____

20..
_____
_____
_____
_____

20..
_____
_____
_____
_____

20..
_____
_____
_____
_____

June 11

Nothing can separate you from God's love, absolutely nothing.
God is enough for time. God is enough for eternity. God is enough!
Hannah Whitall Smith

20..

20..

20..

20..

20..

June 12

For I am persuaded, that neither death, nor life, nor angels, nor principalities, nor powers, nor things present, nor things to come, nor height, nor depth, nor any other creature, shall be able to separate us from the love of God, which is in Christ Jesus our Lord. *Romans 8:38-39 KJV*

20..

20..

20..

20..

20..

June 13

What a beautiful morning! An awesome creation surrounds me – soft breezes, pleasant temperatures, the hills and the valleys evoke praise to the creator of all good things. *Wanda Strange*

20..

20..

20..

20..

20..

June 14
United States of America Flag Day
I pledge allegiance to the Flag of the United States of America, and to the
Republic for which it stands, one Nation under God, indivisible, with
liberty and justice for all.

20..
_____
_____
_____
_____

20..
_____
_____
_____
_____

20..
_____
_____
_____
_____

20..
_____
_____
_____
_____

20..
_____
_____
_____
_____

June 15
Let the wife make the husband glad to come home,
and let him make her sorry to see him leave.
Martin Luther

20.. _____
_____
_____
_____

20.. _____
_____
_____
_____

20.. _____
_____
_____
_____

20.. _____
_____
_____
_____

20.. _____
_____
_____
_____

June 16

Lo, children are an heritage of the LORD: and the fruit of the womb
is his reward. Happy is the man that hath his quiver full of them.
Psalm 127: 3, 5a KJV

20..

20..

20..

20..

20..

June 17

The best remedy for those who are afraid, lonely, or unhappy is to go outside, somewhere where they can be quiet, alone with the heavens, nature, and God, because only then does one feel that all is as it should be.

Anne Frank

20..

20..

20..

20..

20..

June 18

Teach me how to quiet my racing, rising heart
So I might hear the answer You are trying to impart.
Helen Steiner Rice

20..
_____
_____
_____
_____

20..
_____
_____
_____
_____

20..
_____
_____
_____
_____

20..
_____
_____
_____
_____

20..
_____
_____
_____
_____

June 19
Bestow upon us…O Lord our God, understanding to know you,
diligence to seek you, wisdom to find you, and a faithfulness that may
finally embrace you.
Thomas Aquinas

20..

20..

20..

20..

20..

June 20

From the end of the earth will I cry unto thee, when my heart is overwhelmed: lead me to the rock that is higher than I. For thou hast been a shelter for me, and a strong tower from the enemy.

Psalm 61: 2-3 KJV

20..

_____

_____

_____

_____

20..

_____

_____

_____

_____

20..

_____

_____

_____

_____

20..

_____

_____

_____

_____

20..

_____

_____

_____

_____

June 21
He speaks, and the sound of His voice is so sweet the birds hush their singing, and the melody that He gave to me within my heart is ringing.
Charles Austin Miles 1912

20..
_____
_____
_____
_____

20..
_____
_____
_____
_____

20..
_____
_____
_____
_____

20..
_____
_____
_____
_____

20..
_____
_____
_____
_____

June 22

God is not only the answer to a thousand needs. He is the answer to a thousand wants. He is the fulfillment of our chief desire in all of life.
Beth Moore

20..

20..

20..

20..

20..

June 23

Be thou exalted, O God, above the heavens;
let thy glory be above all the earth.
Psalm 57:5 KJV

20__ _____
_____
_____
_____

20__ _____
_____
_____
_____

20__ _____
_____
_____
_____

20__ _____
_____
_____
_____

20__ _____
_____
_____
_____

June 24
Never doubt in the dark
what God has shown you in the light.
Edith Edman

20..
_____
_____
_____
_____

20..
_____
_____
_____
_____

20..
_____
_____
_____
_____

20..
_____
_____
_____
_____

20..
_____
_____
_____
_____

June 25
If nephews and nieces were jewels,
I would have the most beautiful gems ever.
Unknown

20.._____
_____
_____
_____

20.._____
_____
_____
_____

20.._____
_____
_____
_____

20.._____
_____
_____
_____

20.._____
_____
_____
_____

June 26
When you come to the end of your rope,
tie a knot and hang on.
Franklin D. Roosevelt

20..

20..

20..

20..

20..

June 27
Anxiety does not empty tomorrow of its sorrows,
but only empties today of its strength.
Charles Spurgeon

20.. _____
_____
_____
_____

20.. _____
_____
_____
_____

20.. _____
_____
_____
_____

20.. _____
_____
_____
_____

20.. _____
_____
_____
_____

June 28
God, give me grace to accept with serenity the things that cannot be
changed, Courage to change the things which should be changed,
and the Wisdom to distinguish the one from the other.
Reinhold Niebuhr

20..

_____

_____

_____

_____

20..

_____

_____

_____

_____

20..

_____

_____

_____

_____

20..

_____

_____

_____

_____

20..

_____

_____

_____

_____

June 29

And I say unto you, Ask, and it shall be given you; seek, and ye shall
find; knock, and it shall be opened unto you.
Luke 11:9 KJV

20..

20..

20..

20..

20..

June 30

The reality is, my prayers don't change God. But I am convinced prayer changes me. Praying boldly boots me out of that stale place of religious habit into authentic connection with God Himself.

Lysa TerKeurst

20..
_____
_____
_____
_____

20..
_____
_____
_____
_____

20..
_____
_____
_____
_____

20..
_____
_____
_____
_____

20..
_____
_____
_____
_____

July 1
Keep your face to the sun and
you will never see the shadows.
Helen Keller

20.. _____

_____

_____

_____

20.. _____

_____

_____

_____

20.. _____

_____

_____

_____

20.. _____

_____

_____

_____

20.. _____

_____

_____

_____

July 2
Tomorrow is the first blank page of a 365-page book.
Write a good one.
Brad Paisley

20..
_____
_____
_____
_____

20..
_____
_____
_____
_____

20..
_____
_____
_____
_____

20..
_____
_____
_____
_____

20..
_____
_____
_____
_____

July 3
Just living is not enough...
one must have sunshine, freedom, and a little flower.
Hans Christian Andersen

20.._____
_____
_____
_____

20.._____
_____
_____
_____

20.._____
_____
_____
_____

20.._____
_____
_____
_____

20.._____
_____
_____
_____

July 4
United States of America Independence Day
And I'm proud to be an American, where at least I know I'm free.
And I won't forget the men who died, who gave that right to me.
Lee Greenwood

20.. _____
_____
_____
_____

20.. _____
_____
_____
_____

20.. _____
_____
_____
_____

20.. _____
_____
_____
_____

20.. _____
_____
_____
_____

July 5
Our greatest weakness lies in giving up.
The most certain way to succeed is always to try just one more time.
Thomas A. Edison

20..

20..

20..

20..

20..

July 6
Never, never, never
give up
Winston Churchill

20.. _____
_____
_____
_____

20.. _____
_____
_____
_____

20.. _____
_____
_____
_____

20.. _____
_____
_____
_____

20.. _____
_____
_____
_____

July 7
The harder the conflict,
the more glorious the triumph
Thomas Paine

20..

20..

20..

20..

20..

July 8
I attribute my success to this –
I never gave or took any excuse.
Florence Nightingale

20..
_____
_____
_____
_____

20..
_____
_____
_____
_____

20..
_____
_____
_____
_____

20..
_____
_____
_____
_____

20..
_____
_____
_____
_____

July 9
Small deeds done are better than
great deeds planned.
Peter Marshall

20..

20..

20..

20..

20..

July 10

For beautiful eyes, look for the good in others;
for beautiful lips, speak only words of kindness;
and for poise, walk with the knowledge that you are never alone.
Audrey Hepburn

20..
_____
_____
_____
_____

20..
_____
_____
_____
_____

20..
_____
_____
_____
_____

20..
_____
_____
_____
_____

20..
_____
_____
_____
_____

July 11
Together we can change the world,
just one random act of kindness at a time.
Ron Hall

20..

20..

20..

20..

20..

July 12

Any concern too small to be turned into a prayer
is too small to be made into a burden.
Corrie Ten Boom

20..
_____
_____
_____
_____

20..
_____
_____
_____
_____

20..
_____
_____
_____
_____

20..
_____
_____
_____
_____

20..
_____
_____
_____
_____

July 13
I love to think of nature as an unlimited broadcasting station,
through which God speaks to us every hour, if we will only tune in.
George Washington Carver

20..
_____
_____
_____
_____

20..
_____
_____
_____
_____

20..
_____
_____
_____
_____

20..
_____
_____
_____
_____

20..
_____
_____
_____
_____

July 14
True friendship is a plant of slow growth, and must undergo and
withstand the shocks of adversity, before it is entitled to the appellation.
George Washington

20..

20..

20..

20..

20..

July 15
When the storms of life come, if they come to me personally,
to my family or to the world, I want to be strong enough to stand and be
a strength to somebody else, be shelter for somebody else.
Anne Graham Lotz

20..

20..

20..

20..

20..

July 16
We are not cisterns made for hoarding,
we are channels made for sharing.
Billy Graham

20..
_____
_____
_____
_____

20..
_____
_____
_____
_____

20..
_____
_____
_____
_____

20..
_____
_____
_____
_____

20..
_____
_____
_____
_____

July 17
The fellow that has no money is poor.
The fellow that has nothing but money is poorer still.
Billy Sunday

20..
_____
_____
_____
_____

20..
_____
_____
_____
_____

20..
_____
_____
_____
_____

20..
_____
_____
_____
_____

20..
_____
_____
_____
_____

July 18
Life becomes inspiring, not in spite of the problems
and the hard hits, but because of them.
Joni Eareckson Tada

20..
_____
_____
_____
_____

20..
_____
_____
_____
_____

20..
_____
_____
_____
_____

20..
_____
_____
_____
_____

20..
_____
_____
_____
_____

July 19

When thou passest through the waters, I will be with thee; and through
the rivers, they shall not overflow thee: when thou walkest through the
fire, thou shalt not be burned; neither shall the flame kindle upon thee.

Isaiah 43:2 KJV

20..

_____

_____

_____

20..

_____

_____

_____

20..

_____

_____

_____

20..

_____

_____

_____

20..

_____

_____

_____

July 20

God will use whatever he wants to display his glory. Heavens and stars.
History and nations. People and problems.
Max Lucado

20..
_____
_____
_____
_____

20..
_____
_____
_____
_____

20..
_____
_____
_____
_____

20..
_____
_____
_____
_____

20..
_____
_____
_____
_____

July 21
All the great things are simple, and many can be expressed in a
single word: freedom, justice, honor, duty, mercy, hope.
Winston Churchill

20..
_____
_____
_____
_____

20..
_____
_____
_____
_____

20..
_____
_____
_____
_____

20..
_____
_____
_____
_____

20..
_____
_____
_____
_____

July 22

Love recognizes no barriers. It jumps hurdles, leaps fences, penetrates walls to arrive at its destination full of hope.
Maya Angelou

20..
_____
_____
_____
_____

20..
_____
_____
_____
_____

20..
_____
_____
_____
_____

20..
_____
_____
_____
_____

20..
_____
_____
_____
_____

July 23
I dwell in possibility.
Emily Dickinson

20..

20..

20..

20..

20..

July 24

We have always held to the hope, the belief, the conviction
that there is a better life, a better world, beyond the horizon.
Franklin D. Roosevelt

20..
_____
_____
_____
_____

20..
_____
_____
_____
_____

20..
_____
_____
_____
_____

20..
_____
_____
_____
_____

20..
_____
_____
_____
_____

July 25
And now abideth faith, hope, charity, these three;
but the greatest of these is charity.
1 Corinthians 13:13 KJV

20..
_____
_____
_____
_____

20..
_____
_____
_____
_____

20..
_____
_____
_____
_____

20..
_____
_____
_____
_____

20..
_____
_____
_____
_____

July 26
Love is like a beautiful flower which I may not touch,
but whose fragrance makes the garden a place of delight just the same.
Helen Keller

20..

20..

20..

20..

20..

July 27
My faith helps me understand that circumstances
don't dictate my happiness, my inner peace.
Denzel Washington

20..
_____
_____
_____
_____

20..
_____
_____
_____
_____

20..
_____
_____
_____
_____

20..
_____
_____
_____
_____

20..
_____
_____
_____
_____

July 28
Next to the Word of God, the noble art of music
is the greatest treasure in the world.
Martin Luther

20..
_____
_____
_____
_____

20..
_____
_____
_____
_____

20..
_____
_____
_____
_____

20..
_____
_____
_____
_____

20..
_____
_____
_____
._____

July 29
Good books, like good friends, are few and chosen;
the more select, the more enjoyable.
Louisa May Alcott

20..

_____

_____

_____

_____

20..

_____

_____

_____

_____

20..

_____

_____

_____

_____

20..

_____

_____

_____

_____

20..

_____

_____

_____

_____

July 30
People are like stained - glass windows. They sparkle and shine when
the sun is out, but when the darkness sets in, their true beauty is
revealed only if there is a light from within.
Elisabeth Kubler-Ross

20..
_____
_____
_____
_____

20..
_____
_____
_____
_____

20..
_____
_____
_____
_____

20..
_____
_____
_____
_____

20..
_____
_____
_____
_____

July 31
Not that I speak in respect of want: for I have learned,
in whatsoever state I am, therewith to be content.
Philippians 4:11 KJV

20..
_____
_____
_____
_____

20..
_____
_____
_____
_____

20..
_____
_____
_____
_____

20..
_____
_____
_____
_____

20..
_____
_____
_____
_____

August 1
The first fresh hour of every morning should be dedicated to the Lord,
whose mercy gladdens it with golden light.
Charles Spurgeon

20..

_____

_____

_____

_____

20..

_____

_____

_____

_____

20..

_____

_____

_____

_____

20..

_____

_____

_____

_____

20..

_____

_____

_____

_____

August 2

Never be bullied into silence. Never allow yourself to be made a victim.
Accept no one's definition of your life; define yourself.

Robert Frost

20..
_____
_____
_____
_____

20..
_____
_____
_____
_____

20..
_____
_____
_____
_____

20..
_____
_____
_____
_____

20..
_____
_____
_____
_____

August 3

Everybody needs beauty as well as bread, places to
play in and pray in, where nature may heal
and give strength to body and soul.
John Muir

20..

_____

_____

_____

20..

_____

_____

_____

20..

_____

_____

_____

20..

_____

_____

_____

20..

_____

_____

_____

August 4

There is nothing is more musical than a sunset. He who feels what he
sees will find no more beautiful example of development in all that book
which, alas, musicians read but too little - the book of Nature.
Claude Debussy

20..

20..

20..

20..

20..

August 5

Our task must be to free ourselves by widening our circle of compassion
to embrace all living creatures and the whole of nature and its beauty.
Albert Einstein

20..
_____
_____
_____
_____

20..
_____
_____
_____
_____

20..
_____
_____
_____
_____

20..
_____
_____
_____
_____

20..
_____
_____
_____
_____

August 6
Bless the LORD, O my soul: and all that is within me, bless his holy name.
Bless the LORD, O my soul, and forget not all his benefits:
Psalm 103:1-2 KJV

20..

20..

20..

20..

20..

August 7
Walking with a friend in the dark is better
than walking alone in the light.
Helen Keller

20..
_____
_____
_____
_____

20..
_____
_____
_____
_____

20..
_____
_____
_____
_____

20..
_____
_____
_____
_____

20..
_____
_____
_____
_____

August 8
Lord, make me an instrument of thy peace.
Where there is hatred, let me sow love.
Francis of Assisi

20..

20..

20..

20..

20..

August 9
To one who has faith, no explanation is necessary.
To one without faith, no explanation is possible.
Thomas Aquinas

20..
_____
_____
_____
_____

20..
_____
_____
_____
_____

20..
_____
_____
_____
_____

20..
_____
_____
_____
_____

20..
_____
_____
_____
_____

August 10
Faith is taking the first step
even when you don't see the whole staircase.
Martin Luther King, Jr.

20..
_____
_____
_____
_____

20..
_____
_____
_____
_____

20..
_____
_____
_____
_____

20..
_____
_____
_____
_____

20..
_____
_____
_____
_____

August 11
Now faith is the substance of things hoped for,
the evidence of things not seen.
Hebrews 11:1

20..
_____
_____
_____
_____

20..
_____
_____
_____
_____

20..
_____
_____
_____
_____

20..
_____
_____
_____
_____

20..
_____
_____
_____
_____

August 12
Be faithful in small things
because it is in them that your strength lies.
Mother Teresa

20..

20..

20..

20..

20..

August 13

Live your life while you have it. Life is a splendid gift. There is
nothing small in it. Far the greatest things grow by God's law out of
the smallest. But to live your life, you must discipline it.

Florence Nightingale

20..

20..

20..

20..

20..

August 14
My heart is singing for joy this morning! A miracle has happened! The light of understanding has shone upon my little pupil's mind, and behold, all things are changed!
Anne Sullivan

20.._____
_____
_____
_____

20.._____
_____
_____
_____

20.._____
_____
_____
_____

20.._____
_____
_____
_____

20.._____
_____
_____
_____

August 15
If you would be loved,
love and be loveable.
Benjamin Franklin

20..
_____
_____
_____
_____

20..
_____
_____
_____
_____

20..
_____
_____
_____
_____

20..
_____
_____
_____
_____

20..
_____
_____
_____
_____

August 16
My happiness grows in direct proportion to my acceptance,
and in inverse proportion to my expectations.
Michael J. Fox

20..
_____
_____
_____
_____

20..
_____
_____
_____
_____

20..
_____
_____
_____
_____

20..
_____
_____
_____
_____

20..
_____
_____
_____
_____

August 17

At the end of your life, you will never regret not having passed one more test, not winning one more verdict or not closing one more deal. You will regret time not spent with a husband, a friend, a child, or a parent.
Barbara Bush

20..

20..

20..

20..

20..

August 18
There are times I think it might be better to have
my future predictable, but looking back,
I'm always grateful God didn't tell me ahead of time.
Charles Swindoll, Growing Wish in Family Life

20..

_____

_____

_____

20..

_____

_____

_____

20..

_____

_____

_____

20..

_____

_____

_____

20..

_____

_____

_____

August 19

And he (Jesus) said, The things which are impossible with men are
possible with God.
Luke 18:27KJV

20..
_____
_____
_____
_____

20..
_____
_____
_____
_____

20..
_____
_____
_____
_____

20..
_____
_____
_____
_____

20..
_____
_____
_____
_____

August 20

The Bible tells us that whenever we come before God,
whatever our purpose or prayer request,
we are always to come with a thankful heart.
David Jeremiah

20..
_____
_____
_____
_____

20..
_____
_____
_____
_____

20..
_____
_____
_____
_____

20..
_____
_____
_____
_____

20..
_____
_____
_____
_____

August 21
One benefit of summer was that each day
we had more light to read by.
Jeanette Walls, The Glass Castle

20..
_____
_____
_____
_____

20..
_____
_____
_____
_____

20..
_____
_____
_____
_____

20..
_____
_____
_____
_____

20..
_____
_____
_____
_____

August 22

Shall I compare thee to a summer's day? Thou art more lovely and
more temperate: Rough winds do shake the darling buds of May, and
summer's lease has all too short a date.
Sonnet 18, William Shakespeare

20..

20..

20..

20..

20..

August 23
Right now,
God is working all around you.
Henry T. Blackaby, Experiencing God

20..
_____
_____
_____
_____

20..
_____
_____
_____
_____

20..
_____
_____
_____
_____

20..
_____
_____
_____
_____

20..
_____
_____
_____
_____

August 24
A new heart also will I give you, and a new spirit will I put within
you: and I will take away the stony heart out of your flesh,
and I will give you an heart of flesh.
Ezekiel 36:26 KJV

20..

20..

20..

20..

20..

August 25
Hope is the thing with feathers that perches in the soul - and sings the tunes without the words - and never stops at all.
Emily Dickinson

20..
_____
_____
_____
_____

20..
_____
_____
_____
_____

20..
_____
_____
_____
_____

20..
_____
_____
_____
_____

20..
_____
_____
_____
_____

August 26
People may hear your words,
but they feel your attitude.
John C. Maxwell

20..

20..

20..

20..

20..

August 27
Be patient. God is using today's difficulties to strengthen you
for tomorrow. He is equipping you.
The God who makes things grow will help you bear fruit.
Max Lucado

20..
_____
_____
_____
_____

20..
_____
_____
_____
_____

20..
_____
_____
_____
_____

20..
_____
_____
_____
_____

20..
_____
_____
_____
_____

August 28
Every experience in my life provides the opportunity to make a difference in the lives of each person I encounter. I can make a difference, and what I do really matters. *Wanda Strange*

20.._____
_____
_____
_____

20.._____
_____
_____
_____

20.._____
_____
_____
_____

20.._____
_____
_____
_____

20.._____
_____
_____
_____

August 29
The purpose of life is not to be happy. It is to be useful, to be
honorable, to be compassionate, to have it make some difference that
you have lived and lived well.
Ralph Waldo Emerson

20..
_____
_____
_____
_____

20..
_____
_____
_____
_____

20..
_____
_____
_____
_____

20..
_____
_____
_____
_____

20..
_____
_____
_____
_____

August 30

Jesus said unto him, Thou shalt love the Lord thy God with all thy heart, and with all thy soul, and with all thy mind. This is the first and great commandment. And the second is like unto it, Thou shalt love thy neighbour as thyself. *Matthew 22: 37-39 KJV*

20..

_____

_____

_____

20..

_____

_____

_____

20..

_____

_____

_____

20..

_____

_____

_____

20..

_____

_____

_____

August 31
Only God can fully satisfy
the hungry heart of man.
Hugh Black

20..

20..

20..

20..

20..

September 1
How glorious the splendor of a human heart
that trusts that it is loved!
Brennan Manning

20.._____
_____
_____
_____

20.._____
_____
_____
_____

20.._____
_____
_____
_____

20.._____
_____
_____
_____

20.._____
_____
_____
_____

September 2
We often miss opportunity because
it's dressed in overalls and looks like work.
Thomas A. Edison

20..
_____
_____
_____
_____

20..
_____
_____
_____
_____

20..
_____
_____
_____
_____

20..
_____
_____
_____
_____

20..
_____
_____
_____
_____

September 3
Hide not your talents, they for use were made,
What's a sundial in the shade?
Benjamin Franklin

20..

20..

20..

20..

20..

September 4
If there is no struggle,
there is no progress.
Frederick Douglass

20..
_____
_____
_____
_____

20..
_____
_____
_____
_____

20..
_____
_____
_____
_____

20..
_____
_____
_____
_____

20..
_____
_____
_____
_____

September 5

Be strong and of a good courage, fear not, nor be afraid of them:
for the LORD thy God, he it is that doth go with thee;
he will not fail thee, nor forsake thee.
Deuteronomy 31:6 KJV

20.._____

_____

_____

_____

20.._____

_____

_____

_____

20.._____

_____

_____

_____

20.._____

_____

_____

_____

20.._____

_____

_____

_____

September 6
Don't hide a thing. Show God all those hurts.
He's ready to heal every one –
if you're ready to run toward tomorrow.
Come Before Winter, Charles Swindoll

20..
_____
_____
_____
_____

20..
_____
_____
_____
_____

20..
_____
_____
_____
_____

20..
_____
_____
_____
_____

20..
_____
_____
_____
_____

September 7

The massive oak trees in my back yard amaze me. Magnificent, beautiful and strong – standing the test of time – serving as a reminder of the history they have witnessed. *Wanda Strange*

20..

20..

20..

20..

20..

September 8
A quiet morning with a loving God puts the
events of the upcoming day into proper perspective
Janette Oke

20.._____
_____
_____
_____

20.._____
_____
_____
_____

20.._____
_____
_____
_____

20.._____
_____
_____
_____

20.._____
_____
_____
_____

September 9

In all affairs it's a healthy thing now and then to hang
a question mark on the things you have long taken for granted.
Bertrand Russell

20..

20..

20..

20..

20..

September 10

I've learned that people will forget what you said, people will forget
what you did, but people will never forget how you made them feel.
Maya Angelou

20..

_____

_____

_____

_____

20..

_____

_____

_____

_____

20..

_____

_____

_____

_____

20..

_____

_____

_____

_____

20..

_____

_____

_____

_____

September 11
Anyone who stops learning is old, whether at twenty or eighty.
Anyone who keeps learning stays young.
Henry Ford

20..
_____
_____
_____
_____

20..
_____
_____
_____
_____

20..
_____
_____
_____
_____

20..
_____
_____
_____
_____

20..
_____
_____
_____
_____

September 12
Intellectual growth should commence at birth
and cease only at death.
Albert Einstein

20..

20..

20..

20..

20..

September 13
You can never get a cup of tea large enough
or a book long enough to suit me.
C.S. Lewis

20..
_____
_____
_____
_____

20..
_____
_____
_____
_____

20..
_____
_____
_____
_____

20..
_____
_____
_____
_____

20..
_____
_____
_____
_____

September 14
I alone cannot change the world,
but I can cast a stone across the waters to create many ripples.
Mother Teresa

20..

20..

20..

20..

20..

September 15
I have learned that the things that divide us are far less important than those that connect us.
Kitchen Table Wisdom, Rachel Naomi Remen,

20..

20..

20..

20..

20..

September 16
God loves you as though you are the only person in the world,
and He loves everyone the way He loves you.
David Jeremiah

20..
_____
_____
_____
_____

20..
_____
_____
_____
_____

20..
_____
_____
_____
_____

20..
_____
_____
_____
_____

20..
_____
_____
_____
_____

September 17
He that dwelleth in the secret place of the most High shall abide
under the shadow of the Almighty.
Psalm 91:1 KJV

20.._____

_____

_____

_____

20.._____

_____

_____

_____

20.._____

_____

_____

_____

20.._____

_____

_____

_____

20.._____

_____

_____

_____

September 18
The Indian Summer of life should be a little sunny
and a little sad, like the season, and infinite in wealth and depth
of tone, but never hustled.
Henry Adams

20.._____

_____

_____

_____

20.._____

_____

_____

_____

20.._____

_____

_____

_____

20.._____

_____

_____

_____

20.._____

_____

_____

_____

September 19

Don't ever hesitate to take to [God] whatever is on your heart.
He already knows it anyway,
but He doesn't want you to bear its pain or celebrate its joy alone.
Billy Graham

20..

_____

_____

_____

_____

20..

_____

_____

_____

_____

20..

_____

_____

_____

_____

20..

_____

_____

_____

_____

20..

_____

_____

_____

_____

September 20
Autumn…
the year's last, loveliest smile.
William Cullen Bryant

20.. _____
_____
_____
_____

20.. _____
_____
_____
_____

20.. _____
_____
_____
_____

20.. _____
_____
_____
_____

20.. _____
_____
_____
_____

September 21
Give me juicy autumnal fruit,
ripe and red from the orchard.
The Complete Poems, Walt Whitman

20..

20..

20..

20..

20..

September 22

Facts bring us to knowledge, but stories lead to wisdom.
Kitchen Table Wisdom: Stories That Heal,
Rachel Naomi Remen

20..

_____

20..

_____

20..

_____

20..

_____

20..

_____

September 23
One who gains strength by overcoming obstacles
possesses the only strength which can overcome adversity.
Albert Schweitzer

20..

20..

20..

20..

20..

September 24

If we had no winter, the spring would not be so pleasant: if we did not
sometimes taste of adversity, prosperity would not be so welcome.
Meditations Divine and Moral, Anne Bradstreet

20..

___

20..

___

20..

___

20..

___

20..

___

September 25
And we know that all things work together for good
to them that love God, to them who are the called
according to his purpose.
Romans 8:28 KJV

20..
_____
_____
_____
_____

20..
_____
_____
_____
_____

20..
_____
_____
_____
_____

20..
_____
_____
_____
_____

20..
_____
_____
_____
_____

September 26

Beauty is God's handwriting – a wayside sacrament;
welcome it in every fair face, every fair sky,
every fair flower, and thank for it, Him.
Charles Kingsley

20..
_____
_____
_____
_____

20..
_____
_____
_____
_____

20..
_____
_____
_____
_____

20..
_____
_____
_____
_____

20..
_____
_____
_____
_____

September 27

One fall day, I stood in awe of the magnificence of the Grand Canyon. Other days the focus of my gratitude has been the ocean, mighty oaks in my backyard, or the monarchs whose migratory pattern bring them to the zinnias on my back patio. *Wanda Strange*

20..
_____
_____
_____
_____

20..
_____
_____
_____
_____

20..
_____
_____
_____
_____

20..
_____
_____
_____
_____

20..
_____
_____
_____
_____

September 28

The way to happiness: Keep your heart free from hate, your mind from worry. Live simply, expect little, give much. Scatter sunshine, forget self, think of others. Try this for a week and you will be surprised.

Norman Vincent Peale

20..
_____
_____
_____
_____

20..
_____
_____
_____
_____

20..
_____
_____
_____
_____

20..
_____
_____
_____
_____

20..
_____
_____
_____
_____

September 29
F-E-A-R has two meanings: 'Forget Everything and Run' or
'Face Everything and Rise.' The choice is yours.
Zig Ziglar

20..
_____

_____

_____

_____

20..
_____

_____

_____

_____

20..
_____

_____

_____

_____

20..
_____

_____

_____

_____

20..
_____

_____

_____

_____

September 30

I've told you all this so that trusting me, you will be unshakable and assured, deeply at peace. In this godless world you will continue to experience difficulties. But take heart! I've conquered the world.

John 16:33 The Message

20..
_____
_____
_____
_____

20..
_____
_____
_____
_____

20..
_____
_____
_____
_____

20..
_____
_____
_____
_____

20..
_____
_____
_____
_____

October 1

Make regular deposits in your memory bank, to be withdrawn as needed. Sweet recollections provide comfort and strength in times of distress, struggle or grief. *Wanda Strange*

20..
_____
_____
_____
_____

20..
_____
_____
_____
_____

20..
_____
_____
_____
_____

20..
_____
_____
_____
_____

20..
_____
_____
_____
_____

October 2
There are some things you learn best in calm,
and some in storm.
Willa Cather

20..
_____
_____
_____
_____

20..
_____
_____
_____
_____

20..
_____
_____
_____
_____

20..
_____
_____
_____
_____

20..
_____
_____
_____
_____

October 3
Where words fail,
music speaks.
Hans Christian Andersen

20..
_____

20..
_____

20..
_____

20..
_____

20..
_____

October 4
In times like these, it helps to recall
that there have always been times like these.
Paul Harvey

20..
_____
_____
_____
_____

20..
_____
_____
_____
_____

20..
_____
_____
_____
_____

20..
_____
_____
_____
_____

20..
_____
_____
_____
_____

October 5

O sing unto the LORD a new song; for he hath done marvellous things:
his right hand, and his holy arm, hath gotten him the victory.
Psalm 98:1 KJV

20..
_____
_____
_____
_____

20..
_____
_____
_____
_____

20..
_____
_____
_____
_____

20..
_____
_____
_____
_____

20..
_____
_____
_____
_____

October 6
Focus more on your desire than on your doubt,
and the dream will take care of itself
Mark Twain

20..

_____

_____

_____

_____

20..

_____

_____

_____

_____

20..

_____

_____

_____

_____

20..

_____

_____

_____

_____

20..

_____

_____

_____

_____

October 7
We are told to let our light shine, and if it does, we won't need to
tell anybody it does. Lighthouses don't fire cannons
to call attention to their shining- they just shine.
Dwight L Moody

20..

20..

20..

20..

20..

October 8

Earth's crammed with heaven, And every common bush
afire with God: But only he who sees takes off his shoes.
Elizabeth Barrett Browning

20..

20..

20..

20..

20..

October 9
The aim and final end of all music should be none other
than the glory of God and the refreshment of the soul.
Johann Sebastian Bach

20..

20..

20..

20..

20..

October 10

And they sung a new song, saying, Thou art worthy to take the book,
and to open the seals thereof: for thou wast slain, and hast redeemed
us to God by thy blood out of every kindred, and tongue,
and people, and nation; *Revelation 5:9 KJV*

20..

_____

_____

_____

_____

20..

_____

_____

_____

_____

20..

_____

_____

_____

_____

20..

_____

_____

_____

_____

20..

_____

_____

_____

_____

October 11
The life of faith isn't meant for tourists.
It's meant for pilgrims.
Eugene H. Peterson

20..

20..

20..

20..

20..

October 12
How very little can be done
under the spirit of fear
Florence Nightingale

20.. _____
_____
_____
_____

20.. _____
_____
_____
_____

20.. _____
_____
_____
_____

20.. _____
_____
_____
_____

20.. _____
_____
_____
_____

October 13
God has allowed hard things in your life so you can show
the world that your God is great and that knowing Him
brings peace and joy, even when life is hard.
Francis Chan

20..

20..

20..

20..

20..

October 14

Remember that when you leave this earth, you can take with you
nothing that you have received - only what you have given: a full
heart, enriched by honest service, love, sacrifice and courage.
Francis of Assisi

20..

20..

20..

20..

20..

October 15
You cannot change reality, but you can control the manner in which
you look at things. Your attitude is under your own control.
Weed out the negative and focus on the positive!
Helen Steiner Rice

20.. _____
_____
_____
_____

20.. _____
_____
_____
_____

20.. _____
_____
_____
_____

20.. _____
_____
_____
_____

20.. _____
_____
_____
_____

October 16

Kind hearts are the gardens, Kind thoughts are the roots, Kind words
are the flowers, Kind deeds are the fruits, Take care of your garden And
keep out the weeds, Fill it with sunshine, Kind words, and Kind deeds.
Henry Wadsworth Longfellow

20..

20..

20..

20..

20..

October 17

But the fruit of the Spirit is love, joy, peace, longsuffering, gentleness, goodness, faith, meekness, temperance: against such there is no law.
Galatians 5:22-23 KJV

20..

20..

20..

20..

20..

October 18

In EVERY situation and EVERY circumstance of your life,
God is always doing a thousand different things
that you cannot see and you do not know.
John Piper

20..

_____

_____

_____

20..

_____

_____

_____

20..

_____

_____

_____

20..

_____

_____

_____

20..

_____

_____

_____

October 19

God is in control, and therefore in EVERYTHING
I can give thanks - not because of the situation
but because of the One who directs and rules over it.
Kay Arthur

20..

20..

20..

20..

20..

October 20
Stay strong! Your test will become your test-imony,
your mess will become your mess-age.
Max Lucado

20..
_____

20..
_____

20..
_____

20..
_____

20..
_____

October 21
It's a great thing for a man to walk on the moon.
But it's a greater thing for God to walk on the earth.
Neil Armstrong

20..

20..

20..

20..

20..

October 22

There can be no greater gift than that of giving one's time and energy
to help others without expecting anything in return.
Nelson Mandela

20..
_____
_____
_____
_____

20..
_____
_____
_____
_____

20..
_____
_____
_____
_____

20..
_____
_____
_____
_____

20..
_____
_____
_____
_____

October 23
Not every day can be an easy one, nor every day fully happy;
but even a day of tough going and difficulty can be a good day.
Norman Vincent Peale

20..
_____
_____
_____
_____

20..
_____
_____
_____
_____

20..
_____
_____
_____
_____

20..
_____
_____
_____
_____

20..
_____
_____
_____
_____

October 24

Obey God in the things he shows you, and instantly the next thing
is opened up. God will never reveal more truth about himself
until you have obeyed what you know already.
Oswald Chambers

20..
_____
_____
_____
_____

20..
_____
_____
_____
_____

20..
_____
_____
_____
_____

20..
_____
_____
_____
_____

20..
_____
_____
_____
_____

October 25
This is all the inheritance I give to my dear family. The religion of
Christ will give them one which will make them rich indeed.
Patrick Henry

20..
_____
_____
_____
_____

20..
_____
_____
_____
_____

20..
_____
_____
_____
_____

20..
_____
_____
_____
_____

20..
_____
_____
_____
_____

October 26
When we long for life without difficulties,
remind us that oaks grow strong in contrary winds
and diamonds are made under pressure.
Peter Marshall

20..
_____
_____
_____
_____

20..
_____
_____
_____
_____

20..
_____
_____
_____
_____

20..
_____
_____
_____
_____

20..
_____
_____
_____
_____

October 27
My job is to take care of the possible
and to trust God with the impossible.
Ruth Graham

20..
_____
_____
_____
_____

20..
_____
_____
_____
_____

20..
_____
_____
_____
_____

20..
_____
_____
_____
_____

20..
_____
_____
_____
_____

October 28
Take care of your body as if you were going to live forever; and take
care of your soul as if you were going to die tomorrow.
Saint Augustine

20..
_____
_____
_____
_____

20..
_____
_____
_____
_____

20..
_____
_____
_____
_____

20..
_____
_____
_____
_____

20..
_____
_____
_____
_____

October 29

But Jesus beheld them, and said unto them, With men this
is impossible; but with God all things are possible.
Matthew 19:26 KJV

20..

_____

20..

_____

20..

_____

20..

_____

20..

_____

October 30

May the strength of God pilot us, may the wisdom of God instruct us,
may the hand of God protect us, may the word of God direct us.
Be always ours this day and for evermore.
Saint Patrick

20..

20..

20..

20..

20..

October 31
Every hour of every day is
an unspeakably perfect miracle.
Walt Whitman

20..

20..

20..

20..

20..

November 1

Each year in November, I intentionally focus on God's abundant provision. As I reflect on His faithfulness, my awareness of God's goodness grows. *Wanda Strange*

20..

_____

_____

_____

_____

20..

_____

_____

_____

_____

20..

_____

_____

_____

_____

20..

_____

_____

_____

_____

20..

_____

_____

_____

_____

November 2
Unless we stand for something,
we will fall for anything.
Peter Marshall

20..
_____
_____
_____
_____

20..
_____
_____
_____
_____

20..
_____
_____
_____
_____

20..
_____
_____
_____
_____

20..
_____
_____
_____
_____

November 3

As we have therefore opportunity, let us do good unto all men,
especially unto them who are of the household of faith.
Galatians 6:10 KJV

20..
_____
_____
_____
_____

20..
_____
_____
_____
_____

20..
_____
_____
_____
_____

20..
_____
_____
_____
_____

20..
_____
_____
_____
_____

November 4
Right is right, even if everyone is against it,
and wrong is wrong, even if everyone is for it.
William Penn

20..
_____
_____
_____
_____

20..
_____
_____
_____
_____

20..
_____
_____
_____
_____

20..
_____
_____
_____
_____

20..
_____
_____
_____
_____

November 5
When we seek to discover the best in others,
we somehow bring out the best in ourselves.
William Arthur Ward

20..

20..

20..

20..

20..

November 6
When you love what you have,
you have everything you need.
Unknown

20..
_____
_____
_____
_____

20..
_____
_____
_____
_____

20..
_____
_____
_____
_____

20..
_____
_____
_____
_____

20..
_____
_____
_____
_____

November 7
We should certainly count our blessings,
but we should also make our blessings count.
Neal A. Maxwell

20..
_____
_____
_____
_____

20..
_____
_____
_____
_____

20..
_____
_____
_____
_____

20..
_____
_____
_____
_____

20..
_____
_____
_____
_____

November 8
Thanksgiving Day is a jewel, to set in the hearts of honest men; but be careful that you do not take the day, and leave out the gratitude.
E. P Powell

20..
_____
_____
_____
_____

20..
_____
_____
_____
_____

20..
_____
_____
_____
_____

20..
_____
_____
_____
_____

20..
_____
_____
_____
_____

November 9
I am thankful for who I am and what I have.
My thanksgiving is perpetual.
Henry David Thoreau

20..
_____
_____
_____
_____

20..
_____
_____
_____
_____

20..
_____
_____
_____
_____

20..
_____
_____
_____
_____

20..
_____
_____
_____
_____

November 10
What if, today,
we were grateful for everything?
Charlie Brown

20..
_____
_____
_____
_____

20..
_____
_____
_____
_____

20..
_____
_____
_____
_____

20..
_____
_____
_____
_____

20..
_____
_____
_____
_____

November 11
Be present in all things and
thankful for all things.
Maya Angelou

20..
_____
_____
_____
_____

20..
_____
_____
_____
_____

20..
_____
_____
_____
_____

20..
_____
_____
_____
_____

20..
_____
_____
_____
_____

November 12
I believe every human has a finite number of heartbeats.
I don't intend to waste any of mine.
Neil Armstrong

20..

20..

20..

20..

20..

November 13
O give thanks unto the LORD, for he is good:
for his mercy endureth for ever.
Psalm 107:1 KJV

20..

20..

20..

20..

20..

November 14
Always laugh when you can.
It is cheap medicine.
Lord Byron

20..
_____
_____
_____
_____

20..
_____
_____
_____
_____

20..
_____
_____
_____
_____

20..
_____
_____
_____
_____

20..
_____
_____
_____
_____

November 15
The fullness of joy is to
behold God in everything.
Julian of Norwich

20..
_____
_____
_____
_____

20..
_____
_____
_____
_____

20..
_____
_____
_____
_____

20..
_____
_____
_____
_____

20..
_____
_____
_____
_____

November 16
We need Joy as we need air. We need Love as we need water.
We need each other as we need the earth we share.
Maya Angelou

20..
_____
_____
_____
_____

20..
_____
_____
_____
_____

20..
_____
_____
_____
_____

20..
_____
_____
_____
_____

20..
_____
_____
_____
_____

November 17

If you want to get warm you must stand near the fire: if you want to be wet you must get into the water. If you want joy, power, peace, eternal life, you must get close to, or even into, the thing that has them.

C.S. Lewis

20..

20..

20..

20..

20..

November 18
I am especially glad of the divine gift of laughter: it has made the
world human and lovable, despite all its pain and wrong.
W. E. B. DuBois

20..

20..

20..

20..

20..

November 19
My home is in heaven.
I'm just traveling through this world.
Billy Graham

20.. _____
_____
_____
_____

20.. _____
_____
_____
_____

20.. _____
_____
_____
_____

20.. _____
_____
_____
_____

20.. _____
_____
_____
_____

November 20
The LORD is good, a strong hold in the day of trouble;
and he knoweth them that trust in him.
Nahum 1:7 KJV

20..

20..

20..

20..

20..

November 21
You will never know God's strength until
He has supported you in deep waters.
Charles Spurgeon

20..

20..

20..

20..

20..

November 22
Opportunities are like sunrises.
If you wait too long, you miss them.
William Arthur Ward

20..
_____
_____
_____
_____

20..
_____
_____
_____
_____

20..
_____
_____
_____
_____

20..
_____
_____
_____
_____

20..
_____
_____
_____
_____

November 23
When you arise in the morning, think of what a precious privilege
it is to be alive - to breathe, to think, to enjoy, to love.
Marcus Aurelius

20..
_____
_____
_____
_____

20..
_____
_____
_____
_____

20..
_____
_____
_____
_____

20..
_____
_____
_____
_____

20..
_____
_____
_____
_____

November 24

Believe in God like you believe in the sunrise. Not because you
can see it, but because you can see all it touches.
C. S. Lewis

20..
_____
_____
_____
_____

20..
_____
_____
_____
_____

20..
_____
_____
_____
_____

20..
_____
_____
_____
_____

20..
_____
_____
_____
_____

November 25

I expect to pass through life but once. If therefore, there be any kindness I can show, or any good thing I can do to any fellow being, let me do it now, and not defer or neglect it, as I shall not pass this way again.
William Penn

20..

20..

20..

20..

20..

November 26

And God shall wipe away all tears from their eyes; and there shall
be no more death, neither sorrow, nor crying, neither shall there be
any more pain: for the former things are passed away.
Revelation 21: 4 KJV

20..
_____
_____
_____
_____

20..
_____
_____
_____
_____

20..
_____
_____
_____
_____

20..
_____
_____
_____
_____

20..
_____
_____
_____
_____

November 27

When we all get to heaven, what a day of rejoicing that will be!
When we all see Jesus, we'll sing and shout the victory.
E. E. Hewitt (1898)

20..

_____

_____

_____

_____

20..

_____

_____

_____

_____

20..

_____

_____

_____

_____

20..

_____

_____

_____

_____

20..

_____

_____

_____

November 28
Every time you smile at someone, it is an action of love,
a gift to that person, a beautiful thing.
Mother Teresa

20..

20..

20..

20..

20..

November 29
Has this world been so kind to you that you should leave with regret?
There are better things ahead than any we leave behind.
C. S. Lewis

20..
_____
_____
_____
_____

20..
_____
_____
_____
_____

20..
_____
_____
_____
_____

20..
_____
_____
_____
_____

20..
_____
_____
_____
_____

November 30

The unthankful heart... discovers no mercies; but let the thankful heart
sweep through the day and, as the magnet finds the iron,
so it will find, in every hour, some heavenly blessings!
Henry Ward Beecher

20..
_____
_____
_____
_____

20..
_____
_____
_____
_____

20..
_____
_____
_____
_____

20..
_____
_____
_____
_____

20..
_____
_____
_____
_____

December 1

The celebration of Advent is possible only to those who are troubled
in soul, who know themselves to be poor and imperfect,
and who look forward to something greater to come.
Dietrich Bonhoeffer

20..

20..

20..

20..

20..

December 2
Let every heart
prepare him room.
Isaac Watts 1719

20..
_____
_____
_____
_____

20..
_____
_____
_____
_____

20..
_____
_____
_____
_____

20..
_____
_____
_____
_____

20..
_____
_____
_____
_____

December 3

Hope has two beautiful daughters; their names are
Anger and Courage. Anger at the way things are,
and Courage to see that they do not remain as they are.
Saint Augustine

20..
_____
_____
_____
_____

20..
_____
_____
_____
_____

20..
_____
_____
_____
_____

20..
_____
_____
_____
_____

20..
_____
_____
_____
_____

December 4

Why art thou cast down, O my soul? and why art thou
disquieted in me? Hope thou in God:
for I shall yet praise him for the help of his countenance.
Psalm 42:5 KJV

20..

_____

_____

_____

_____

20..

_____

_____

_____

_____

20..

_____

_____

_____

_____

20..

_____

_____

_____

_____

20..

_____

_____

_____

_____

December 5
God of hope, I look to you with an open heart and yearning spirit.
During this Advent season, I will keep alert and awake, listening for
your word and keeping to your precepts. My hope is in you.
Mathew Kelly

20..
_____
_____
_____
_____

20..
_____
_____
_____
_____

20..
_____
_____
_____
_____

20..
_____
_____
_____
_____

20..
_____
_____
_____
_____

December 6
The Word became flesh and blood,
and moved into the neighborhood.
John 1:14 The Message

20..
_____
_____
_____
_____

20..
_____
_____
_____
_____

20..
_____
_____
_____
_____

20..
_____
_____
_____
_____

20..
_____
_____
_____
_____

December 7
Peace cannot be achieved through violence,
it can only be attained through understanding.
Ralph Waldo Emerson

20..

20..

20..

20..

20..

December 8
While you are proclaiming peace with your lips,
be careful to have it even more fully in your heart.
Frances of Assisi

20..

20..

20..

20..

20..

December 9
Let there be peace on earth,
and let it begin with me.
Jill Jackson and Sy Miller

20..
_____
_____
_____
_____

20..
_____
_____
_____
_____

20..
_____
_____
_____
_____

20..
_____
_____
_____
_____

20..
_____
_____
_____
_____

December 10

And Mary said, My soul doth magnify the Lord, And my spirit hath rejoiced in God my Saviour…For he that is mighty hath done to me great things; and holy is his name.

Luke 1:46-47,49 KJV

20..

_____

_____

_____

_____

20..

_____

_____

_____

_____

20..

_____

_____

_____

_____

20..

_____

_____

_____

_____

20..

_____

_____

_____

_____

December 11
I have held many things in my hands, and I have lost them all; but
whatever I have placed in God's hands, that I still possess.
Martin Luther

20..
_____
_____
_____
_____

20..
_____
_____
_____
_____

20..
_____
_____
_____
_____

20..
_____
_____
_____
_____

20..
_____
_____
_____
_____

December 12

For unto us a child is born, unto us a son is given: and the government shall be upon his shoulder: and his name shall be called Wonderful, Counsellor, The mighty God, The everlasting Father The Prince of Peace. *Isaiah 9:6*

20..

20..

20..

20..

20..

December 13

These things I have spoken unto you, that in me ye might have peace.
In the world ye shall have tribulation: but be of good cheer; I have
overcome the world. *Jesus Christ –*
John 16:33 KJV

20..
_____
_____
_____
_____

20..
_____
_____
_____
_____

20..
_____
_____
_____
_____

20..
_____
_____
_____
_____

20..
_____
_____
_____
_____

December 14
If you're sincerely seeking God,
God will make His existence evident to you.
William Lane Craig

20..
_____
_____
_____
_____

20..
_____
_____
_____
_____

20..
_____
_____
_____
_____

20..
_____
_____
_____
_____

20..
_____
_____
_____
_____

December 15
Glory to God in the highest,
and on earth peace, good will toward men.
Luke 2:14 KJV

20..
_____
_____
_____
_____

20..
_____
_____
_____
_____

20..
_____
_____
_____
_____

20..
_____
_____
_____
_____

20..
_____
_____
_____
_____

December 16
I will honor Christmas in my heart and
try to keep it all the year.
Charles Dickens

20..

20..

20..

20..

20..

December 17
Joy to the world,
the Lord has come.
Isaac Watts 1719

20..

_____

_____

_____

_____

20..

_____

_____

_____

_____

20..

_____

_____

_____

_____

20..

_____

_____

_____

_____

20..

_____

_____

_____

_____

December 18
Hark the herald angels sing, glory to the newborn King.
Peace on earth and mercy mild. God and sinners reconciled.
Charles Wesley 1739

20..

20..

20..

20..

20..

December 19
Rejoice in the. Lord always:
and again I say, Rejoice.
Philippians 4:4 KJV

20..
_____
_____
_____
_____

20..
_____
_____
_____
_____

20..
_____
_____
_____
_____

20..
_____
_____
_____
_____

20..
_____
_____
_____
_____

December 20
If we could condense all the truths of Christmas into only three words,
these would be the words: GOD WITH US.
John MacArthur

20..
_____
_____
_____
_____

20..
_____
_____
_____
_____

20..
_____
_____
_____
_____

20..
_____
_____
_____
_____

20..
_____
_____
_____
_____

December 21

For God so loved the world, that he gave his only begotten Son,
that whosoever believeth in him should not perish,
but have everlasting life.
John 3:16 KJV

20..
_____
_____
_____
_____

20..
_____
_____
_____
_____

20..
_____
_____
_____
_____

20..
_____
_____
_____
_____

20..
_____
_____
_____
_____

December 22
God's gifts put
man's best dreams to shame.
Elizabeth Barrett Browning

20.. _____
_____
_____
_____

20.. _____
_____
_____
_____

20.. _____
_____
_____
_____

20.. _____
_____
_____
_____

20.. _____
_____
_____
_____

December 23

This is Christmas; not the tinsel, not the giving and receiving,
not even the carols, but the humble heart that receives anew
the wondrous gift, the Christ.
Frank McKibben

20..
_____
_____
_____
_____

20..
_____
_____
_____
_____

20..
_____
_____
_____
_____

20..
_____
_____
_____
_____

20..
_____
_____
_____
_____

December 24
Thanks be unto God for
his unspeakable gift.
2 Corinthians 9:15 KJV

20.._____
_____
_____
_____

20.._____
_____
_____
_____

20.._____
_____
_____
_____

20.._____
_____
_____
_____

20.._____
_____
_____
_____

December 25
I heard the bells on Christmas Day their old, familiar carols play, and
wild and sweet the words repeat of peace on earth, good-will to men!
Henry Wadsworth Longfellow 1863

20..
_____
_____
_____
_____

20..
_____
_____
_____
_____

20..
_____
_____
_____
_____

20..
_____
_____
_____
_____

20..
_____
_____
_____
_____

December 26

Christmas is forever, not for just one day, for loving, sharing, giving,
are not to put away like bells and lights and tinsel, in some box upon a
shelf. The good you do for others is good you do yourself.

Norman Wesley Brooks

20..

_____

_____

_____

_____

20..

_____

_____

_____

_____

20..

_____

_____

_____

_____

20..

_____

_____

_____

_____

20..

_____

_____

_____

_____

December 27

Where do we go when our hope runs low? Because we live in a broken world, our hope will run low. When my hope dwindles, I focus on Christ, my source of hope… When I maintain the proper focus, my heart overflows with gratitude. *Wanda Strange*

20..
_____
_____
_____
_____

20..
_____
_____
_____
_____

20..
_____
_____
_____
_____

20..
_____
_____
_____
_____

20..
_____
_____
_____
_____

December 28
For last year's words belong to last year's language.
And next year's words await another voice.
And to make an end is to make a beginning.
T.S. Eliot

20..
_____
_____
_____
_____

20..
_____
_____
_____
_____

20..
_____
_____
_____
_____

20..
_____
_____
_____
_____

20..
_____
_____
_____
_____

December 29
Great is the art of beginning,
but greater is the art of ending.
Henry Wadsworth Longfellow

20..
_____
_____
_____
_____

20..
_____
_____
_____
_____

20..
_____
_____
_____
_____

20..
_____
_____
_____
_____

20..
_____
_____
_____
_____

December 30
The woods are lovely dark and deep, but I have promises to keep, and miles to go before I sleep, and miles to go before I sleep.
Robert Frost

20..
_____

20..
_____

20..
_____

20..
_____

20..
_____

December 31

Brethren, I count not myself to have apprehended: but this one thing I do, forgetting those things which are behind, and reaching forth unto those things which are before, I press toward the mark for the prize of the high calling of God in Christ Jesus. *Philippians* 3:13-14 KJV

20..

20..

20..

20..

20..

O Lᴏʀᴅ, our Lord, how excellent is thy name in all the earth! who hast set thy glory above the heavens.

Out of the mouth of babes and sucklings hast thou ordained strength because of thine enemies, that thou mightest still the enemy and the avenger.

When I consider thy heavens, the work of thy fingers, the moon and the stars, which thou hast ordained;
What is man, that thou art mindful of him? and the son of man, that thou visitest him?

For thou hast made him a little lower than the angels, and hast crowned him with glory and honour.
Thou madest him to have dominion over the works of thy hands; thou hast put all things under his feet:
All sheep and oxen, yea, and the beasts of the field;
The fowl of the air, and the fish of the sea, and whatsoever passeth through the paths of the seas.

O Lᴏʀᴅ our Lord, how excellent is thy name in all the earth!

Psalm 8 KJV

ABOUT THE AUTHOR

A native Texan, Wanda Strange resides with her husband, Kerry, in Bluff Dale, Texas. Married since 1969, they are the parents of an adult daughter, Ginger. Though Wanda retired from a career in oncology nursing in 2016, experiences with colleagues, patients and caregivers taught her the value of gratitude as a coping mechanism. Her love of people fuels a desire to serve others. She enjoys music, movies, books, and passionately pursues time with family and friends. Participation in a variety of activities enrich this season of life. Faith – family – friends comprise the priorities of Wanda's busy life.

Made in the USA
Columbia, SC
05 October 2020